Reading Power

Women Who Shaped History

Eleanor Roosevelt
More Than a First Lady

Joanne Mattern

The Rosen Publishing Group's
PowerKids Press™
New York

Published in 2003 by The Rosen Publishing Group, Inc.
29 East 21st Street, New York, NY 10010

First Edition

Book Design: Erica Clendening

Photo Credits: Cover © Leo Rosenthal/Timepix; pp. 4, 5, 7, 9, 13, 16, 17 courtesy Franklin D. Roosevelt Library; pp. 5 (inset), 15 Library of Congress, Prints and Photographs; p. 11 © Bradford Bachrach/Timepix; p. 14 © Timepix; pp. 18–19 courtesy of the United Nations; p. 20 © AP/Wide World Photos; p. 21 © Charles Moore/Black Star/Timepix

Library of Congress Cataloging-in-Publication Data

Mattern, Joanne, 1963-
Eleanor Roosevelt : more than a First Lady / Joanne Mattern.
    p. cm. — (Women who shaped history)
Summary: A brief biography of the First Lady, spouse of Franklin D. Roosevelt, who is particularly known for her work for human rights.
Includes bibliographical references and index.
ISBN 0-8239-6501-5 (lib. bdg.)
1. Roosevelt, Eleanor, 1884-1962—Juvenile literature. 2. Presidents' spouses—United States—Biography—Juvenile literature. [1. Roosevelt, Eleanor, 1884-1962. 2. First ladies. 3. Women—Biography.] I. Title.
E807.1.R48 M33 2003
973.917'092—dc21

                                                    2002000517

Contents

The Early Years

Eleanor Roosevelt was one of the most important women of the twentieth century. She worked for things that she believed in. She helped change the lives of many people.

Anna Eleanor Roosevelt was born in New York City on October 11, 1884, to Elliott and Anna Hall Roosevelt. Both of her parents died by the time she was ten. Then, she went to live with her grandmother. In 1899, her grandmother sent her to school in England.

Eleanor Roosevelt enjoyed her time at school in England.

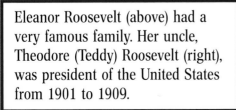

Eleanor Roosevelt (above) had a very famous family. Her uncle, Theodore (Teddy) Roosevelt (right), was president of the United States from 1901 to 1909.

When Eleanor Roosevelt was eighteen years old, she moved back to New York City. She worked as a volunteer in a settlement house. A settlement house is a place for immigrants and poor families to learn new things. She taught dance and exercise classes. She also learned about the problems these families had.

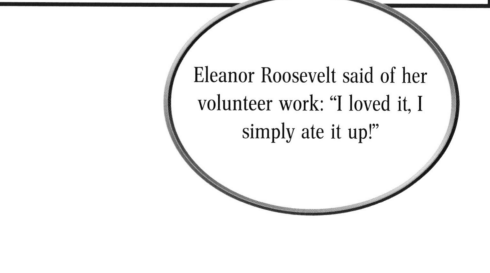

Eleanor Roosevelt said of her volunteer work: "I loved it, I simply ate it up!"

Eleanor Roosevelt was very shy when she was young.

Married Life

In 1905, Eleanor Roosevelt married Franklin Delano Roosevelt, a distant cousin. They had six children.

Franklin Roosevelt was the senator for New York State from 1911 to 1913. As his wife, Eleanor Roosevelt was expected to go to many parties and other events. However, she wanted to do more. Eleanor Roosevelt started working as a volunteer for the Red Cross.

Eleanor Roosevelt (reading book) enjoyed spending time with her family.

Eleanor and Franklin Roosevelt were married on March 17, 1905.

In 1921, Franklin Roosevelt got sick with an illness called polio. He couldn't stand or walk without help. Eleanor Roosevelt helped her husband at home and at work.

"Franklin's illness proved to be a blessing in disguise, for it gave him strength and courage he had not had before."

—Eleanor Roosevelt

Franklin Roosevelt didn't let his illness stop him from working. In 1929, he became governor of New York.

Eleanor Roosevelt also worked to gain rights for women. She worked for other causes, too, such as making laws to keep workers safe.

The First Lady

In 1932, Franklin Roosevelt was elected president of the United States. Eleanor Roosevelt became the first lady.

She did more work than most other first ladies. Franklin Roosevelt couldn't travel much because of his illness. Eleanor Roosevelt traveled across America to help him. She told her husband how Americans lived and what they needed.

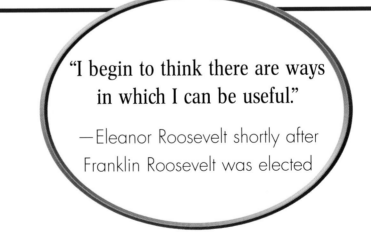

"I begin to think there are ways in which I can be useful."

—Eleanor Roosevelt shortly after Franklin Roosevelt was elected

Eleanor Roosevelt was first lady for 12 years, the longest anyone has ever been first lady.

Eleanor Roosevelt (center, standing) was the president's "eyes and ears."

Eleanor Roosevelt saw that many African Americans were treated unfairly. She often spoke out against racism.

Many magazines and newspapers wrote about Eleanor Roosevelt.

Eleanor Roosevelt also held many press conferences. Often, she asked that only women reporters come. This made some news companies hire women to go to the conferences.

Eleanor Roosevelt spoke to many people about the problems in America.

"My Day"

From 1935 to 1962, Eleanor Roosevelt wrote a daily newspaper column called "My Day." She wrote about equal rights for all people, current events, and more. Millions of Americans read her column.

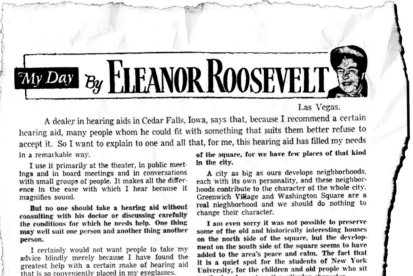

My Day By ELEANOR ROOSEVELT

Las Vegas.

A dealer in hearing aids in Cedar Falls, Iowa, says that, because I recommend a certain hearing aid, many people whom he could fit with something that suits them better refuse to accept it. So I want to explain to one and all that, for me, this hearing aid has filled my needs in a remarkable way.

I use it primarily at the theater, in public meetings and in board meetings and in conversations with small groups of people. It makes all the difference in the ease with which I hear because it magnifies sound.

But no one should take a hearing aid without consulting with his doctor or discussing carefully the conditions for which he needs help. One thing may well suit one person and another thing another person.

I certainly would not want people to take my advice blindly merely because I have found the greatest help with a certain make of hearing aid that is so conveniently placed in my eyeglasses.

I am grateful to the gentleman from Iowa for drawing this situation to my attention. It had never occurred to me that people would do more than try something that I had found good, naturally bearing in mind that their needs might be different and would be concerned only with what best suits their needs.

*   *   *

I appeared at a hearing during the week on the proposed changes in New York's Washington Square, which I hope very much will remain just as it is.

It does not seem to me important that Fifth Av. be extended below where it now begins. What does seem important is preserving the peace and quiet of the square, for we have few places of that kind in the city.

A city as big as ours develops neighborhoods, each with its own personality, and these neighborhoods contribute to the character of the whole city. Greenwich Village and Washington Square are a real nieghborhood and we should do nothing to change their character.

I am even sorry it was not possible to preserve some of the old and historically interesting houses on the north side of the square, but the development on the south side of the square seems to have added to the area's peace and calm. The fact that it is a quiet spot for the students of New York University, for the children and old people who sit on the benches, gives it particular character.

Our passion for destroying and rebuilding everywhere should be curtailed somewhat so that we do preserve a few spots that remain more or less the same and can be revisited and evoke past history.

I have always liked to walk down some of the streets surrounding the square and remember the stories that an old lady, a cousin of mine named Mrs. Weekes, told me when she came to that neighborhood. Her husband did not think it proper for her to go out alone and carry her market basket, so he carried the basket and she clung to his arm while they purchased the household needs for the day. This same old lady had danced with Lafayette!

NEW YORK POST, SUNDAY, MAY 18, 1958   M 7

Eleanor Roosevelt's "My Day" column

Eleanor Roosevelt enjoyed writing.
She wrote about many subjects.

The Later Years

In 1945, Franklin Roosevelt died. Vice President Harry Truman became president.

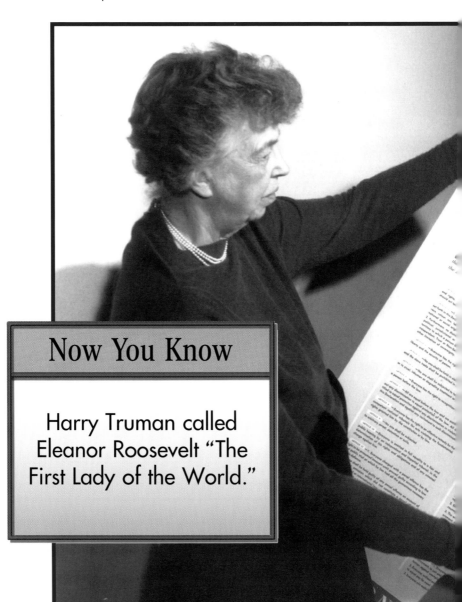

Now You Know

Harry Truman called Eleanor Roosevelt "The First Lady of the World."

Although Eleanor Roosevelt was no longer first lady, she continued to work for the country. She became a United States representative to the United Nations. She worked for peace and human rights.

At the United Nations, Eleanor Roosevelt worked for the rights of people around the world.

Eleanor Roosevelt died on November 7, 1962. She was seventy-eight years old. Eleanor made a difference in the lives of millions of people. She will be remembered for her work as first lady and much more.

"I learned that true happiness lies in doing something useful with your life."

—Eleanor Roosevelt

Time Line

October 11, 1884
Anna Eleanor Roosevelt is born in New York City

1906 *Daughter Anna is born*

1909 *Son, the first Franklin Delano, Jr., is born (he died a few months later)*

1914 *Son, the second Franklin Delano, Jr., is born*

1921 *Franklin Roosevelt becomes sick with polio*

1905 *Marries Franklin Roosevelt*

1907 *Son James is born*

1910 *Son Elliott is born*

1916 *Son John is born*

In 1961, Eleanor Roosevelt worked with President John F. Kennedy for the Peace Corps and for women's rights.

1935 *Begins writing a newspaper column, "My Day"*

November 7, 1962
Eleanor Roosevelt dies

1932 *Franklin Delano Roosevelt is elected president of the United States; Eleanor Roosevelt becomes first lady*

1945 *Franklin Roosevelt dies; Eleanor Roosevelt represents the U.S. at the United Nations*

Glossary

causes (**kawz**-uhz) ideas or goals that many people care about

distant cousin (**dihs**-tuhnt **kuhz**-uhn) the children of your grandparent's brother, sister, or other family member

first lady (**fuhrst lay**-dee) the wife of the U.S. president

immigrants (**ihm**-ih-gruhnts) people who come into a country to live there

newspaper column (**nooz**-pay-puhr **kahl**-uhm) writing by a special person that is printed regularly in a newspaper

polio (**poh**-lee-oh) an illness that makes muscles unable to move

press conference (**prehs kahn**-fuhr-uhns) a meeting for reporters that is given by a public speaker

racism (**ray**-sihz-uhm) judging people based on how they look or the color of their skin

Red Cross (**rehd craws**) a group of people that helps others

representative (rehp-rih-**zen**-tuh-tihv) a person chosen to stand or act for others

rights (**ryts**) things the law says that a person is allowed to do

United Nations (yoo-**ny**-tihd **nay**-shuhnz) a group of countries that work together for peace, understanding, and world change

volunteer (vahl-uhn-**tihr**) someone who works without pay

Resources

Books

Eleanor Everywhere:
The Life of Eleanor Roosevelt
by Monica Kulling
Random House (1999)

Stateswoman to the World:
A Story About Eleanor Roosevelt
by Maryanne N. Weidt
Lerner Publishing Group (1992)

Web Sites

Due to the changing nature of Internet links, PowerKids
Press has developed an on-line list of Web sites related
to the subjects of this book. This site is updated regularly.
Please use this link to access the list:

http://www.powerkidslinks.com/wsh/eler/

Index

Word Count: 460

Note to Librarians, Teachers, and Parents

If reading is a challenge, Reading Power is a solution! Reading Power is perfect for readers who want high-interest subject matter at an accessible reading level. These fact-filled, photo-illustrated books are designed for readers who want straightforward vocabulary, engaging topics, and a manageable reading experience. With clear picture/text correspondence, leveled Reading Power books put the reader in charge. Now readers have the power to get the information they want and the skills they need in a user-friendly format.